Monk Dancers
of Tibet

MONK DANCERS OF TIBET

TEXT AND PHOTOGRAPHS BY

Matthieu Ricard

Translated by Charles Hastings

SHAMBHALA · *Boston & London* · 2003

For Shechen Rabjam Rinpoche

CONTENTS

Copyright information on page 128

A People Bears Witness

Without fear, without second thoughts, and without effort, let flow from the space of mind the divine gestures and movements of unknown dances and unheard chants.

TANTRA OF THE WHEEL OF TIME

THE VERY notion of dancing monks might seem strange. In the West dancing is often an expression of sensual exuberance, sometimes with a connotation of seduction far removed from monastic contemplation. Secular dancing and music are even excluded by Buddhist monastic rules. Sacred dance has a different basis. Although it is certainly an expression of joy, that joy does not comes from arousing emotions, but from pacifying them. When the monks dance they are meditating, and at the same time offering a spiritual gift to the lay community that lives in symbiosis with their monastery. Through symbolic gesture and sacred sound, they transmit an experience that is the culmination of long contemplative ceremonies. It is said that this kind of dance liberates by seeing, just as sacred music liberates through hearing, the blessing of a spiritual master liberates through touch, imbibing sacred substances liberates by taste, and meditation liberates by thought. "Liberate" here means to liberate from the bondage of the five mental poisons that destroy inner peace—hatred, covetousness, ignorance, pride and jealousy.

That is the traditional understanding of the sacred dances that originated in India and flourished for centuries in Tibet. They are now preserved in exile in India, Nepal, and Bhutan, and have been presented in the West, by the monks of Shechen and other Tibetan monasteries, in the same spirit of sharing a profound inner experience.

The origin of sacred dance, or *cham*, goes back to the ninth century when Guru Padmasambhava introduced Buddhism in Tibet. Through the ages this practice has been enriched and renewed on the basis of visionary indications received by certain great masters. In the context of sacred art, innovations are not invented, but flow from the wealth of visionary experience which accompanies deep spiritual realization. Thus the dance forms first appear in the mind of a spiritually advanced individual and are transmitted as accurately as possible by his disciples from generation to generation.

After the Chinese invasion of Tibet in 1959, over six thousand monasteries were razed to the ground. A million Tibetans perished, a sixth of the total population. The libraries were burnt or thrown into the rivers, the statues broken up or melted down to make cannons and rifles. For example, in 1985 when we visited Shechen, a great monastery of Eastern Tibet, only a few stones were left standing. Nonetheless, the famous annual dance festival of Shechen was revived that year amidst the ruins, and since then the monastery has been partially restored. A branch monastery of Shechen has been built in Nepal by Dilgo Khyentse Rinpoche. The work began in 1980, and for ten years builders, stonecutters, sculptors, jewelers, and tailors have made this branch of Shechen one of the most beautiful examples of Tibetan art in exile. A dance master and a chanting master from Tibet spent several years in Katmandu transmitting the musical and choreographic tradition for which the mother monastery was famous. The dance festival, which takes place on the tenth day of the second lunar month (March–April) is one of the great events of the year and attracts thousands of devotees.

The sacred dances of the land of snows are not only an act of spiritual sharing. They are also the witness of a people who have already undergone a real human genocide and are now experiencing cultural genocide. By opening a window on the sacred world of the monks, the dances allow us to discover an aspect of the vitality of Tibetan religion, and show us that even if, as the Dalai Lama often says, Tibet does not have oil to run cars, it has "oil" for the mind.

Tibet's culture is still alive. It is not just the legacy of six million Tibetans but an element in a world heritage that it is our duty to preserve.

SACRED LAND,

The mudra of the dance is a reflection in the mirror of enlightenment.

LOCHEN DHARMASHRI

BUDDHISM appeared in India in the sixth century B.C.E., when Prince Siddhartha attained supreme knowledge and thus became the Buddha Shakyamuni, the awakened one. From the age of thirty until his death at the age of eighty the Buddha constantly taught his innumerable disciples. The variety of his teachings and the diversity of their levels of meaning reflect the multitude of different characters and capacities of beings and the diversity of the methods needed to guide them to enlightenment.

It is said that the Buddha manifested to certain particularly gifted disciples in the form of various deities, such as *Kalachakra* (Wheel of Time) and *Guhyasamaj* (Matrix of Secrets), to enable them to progress rapidly on the spiritual path using exceptional techniques of meditation. At that time Buddha also manifested as wrathful deities, whose awesome appearance symbolizes the invincible power of compassion. Those deities danced in a thousand majestic ways, symbolizing the innumerable aspects of their activity to help beings.

LAND OF EXILE

This, it is said, is how the sacred dances came into being in India. They were danced at spiritual feasts known as *ganachakra*. During these gatherings the initiates would dance spontaneously, without hesitation or inhibition. Over the years the dances came to be codified: they were taught to the adepts and their significance was explained. An uninterrupted transmission from teacher to disciple, enriched by the experience of great meditators, has faithfully maintained the continuity of this practice.

Buddhism did not reach Tibet until the fifth century C.E., when the king Lhatori Nyentsen first introduced a collection of the Buddha's teachings. And it was not until the time of the kings Songtsen Gampo and Trisong Detsen (742–787?) that Buddhism really spread throughout the land. King Trisong Detsen invited the Indian abbot Shantarakshita to found a great monastery. Shantarakshita strove in vain to subdue the negative forces and mountain spirits hostile to the propagation of the dharma, as the teaching of the Buddha

is known. The abbot declared finally that only Padmasambhava, the "Lotus-Born," could succeed in the task. This powerful tantric master, also known as Guru Rinpoche, "Precious Master," is revered by Tibetans as the second Buddha. He came from Uddiyana (in the present valley of Swat in the north of Pakistan). He traveled to India, and subsequently to Tibet, where he established Buddhism on a firm basis. He built and consecrated Samye, the first monastery. Then he transmitted to the king and numerous other disciples the initiations of the Vajrayana along with their pith instructions. Under his direction Tibetan scholars aided by Indian pandits translated the *Tripitaka* ("three baskets," the three sections of the Buddha's teachings), into Tibetan, as well as innumerable tantras, commentaries, and ritual texts. The spiritual lineage of Padmasambhava is called the Ancient Tradition (Nyingma), because it was the sole guardian of Tibetan Buddhism from the ninth to eleventh centuries. The "new" orders, Sakya, Kagyu, and Geluk, flourished

initiated his disciples in the meditation on a particular mandala (a symbolic representation of the universe and its inhabitants), and having given them all the necessary instructions, Padmasambhava entrusted them with those teachings in the form of parchments written in symbolic language which he hid in the sky, the earth, a rock, a lake, or a sacred image. He would designate one of his disciples present at that moment as the inheritor of a particular spiritual treasure, predicting at what time, in what place, and in what circumstances an incarnation of that disciple would reveal the treasure to benefit the beings of his era. The tradition of "revealed treasures" (*terma*) has played an important role in the development of Tibetan Buddhism right up to the present day. Such revealed teachings are considered to have a particular potency because they are specifically adapted to the epoch in which they appear.

A number of these treasures contain instructions for new forms of sacred dance. The best known is that of Guru Chöwang (1212–1270). In a vision he found himself riding a white horse that carried him aloft through the air to the glorious copper-colored mountain, the paradise of Padmasambhava. There he met Padmasambhava's eight manifestations and received teaching from them on the nature of mind. He also saw a vast gathering of celestial beings dancing

from the eleventh century onward on the basis of new translations of Sanskrit texts.

When Padmasambhava was preparing to consecrate the site of the monastery of Samye he rose into the air and subdued the spirits of the ground with a majestic dance. The story goes that the area where his shadow fell on the ground marked the boundaries of the monastery. This event was subsequently commemorated by dances linked to the deity Vajrakilaya, a tradition that still continues today.

The Visionary Source

The visions on which the dances are based are usually the exploits of masters known as "treasure revealers" (*tertön*), who are considered to be emanations of the disciples of Padmasambhava. Having

Padmasambhava and his eight manifestations, at the Shechen monastery.

before the master. After this transforming experience he inaugurated the festival of the tenth day, which celebrates in dance the coming to Tibet of Padmasambhava and the establishment of Buddhism.

This process of new dances being created as a result of visionary experiences was to be repeated again and again over the centuries. Thus the great Bhutanese treasure revealer Pema Lingpa (1450–1521) had a dream in which Yeshe Tsogyel, queen of Tibet and

also the principal consort and spiritual disciple of Padmasambhava, said: "This is the way to dance the ritual of the Rain of Blessings." She showed him the dance of the five *dakinis* (feminine deities, literally "travelers in the sky of wisdom"). When Pema Lingpa awoke he clearly remembered the images of the dance. During the following days he had other visions containing complementary instructions. He taught himself to execute the movements and then transmitted them to his disciples. On another

occasion, when he was about to consecrate a temple, sages appeared to him, saying, "This is the way to dance when consecrating a sanctuary." He taught the new movements to his disciples, who danced them for the consecration of the temple of Tamchin in Bumthang province, Bhutan.

Such experiences sometimes take the form of miraculous events. In the biography of Tsangpa Gyare, a sage of the twelfth century, we read:

"When the great hermit Tsangpa

place and made it promise to help all practitioners of the Dharma. The rock bearing the hand- and footprints of Tsangpa Gyare can still be seen to this day."

In the sixteenth century the great teacher Khamtrul Kunga Tenzin, in retreat in a mountain hermitage, had a vision in which the whole universe became the pure land of Padmasambhava, a true mandala. First he saw it in two dimensions, then in three dimensions, until he could perceive all the details at the same time. Padmasambhava, radiant with compassion, told Kunga Tenzin to leave his retreat and work for the benefit of beings, saying: "You are dwelling in a cave called the Vulture's Nest. Now it is time to fly into the world." During this vision Kunga Tenzin also saw wonderful dances. Padmasambhava told him: "Teach these dances, for they will bring great blessings to those who see them." This was the beginning of the Gar Cham, a dance festival that took place at Khampagar in eastern Tibet. It continues today at Tashijong in northern India.

The way highly realized masters can inspire their disciples is shown by the following story. Once, when the annual dance festival was approaching, Tutop Lingpa told the monks of his monastery not to practice for the event in advance. When the day came, he told them to simply dance whatever they felt. Then

Gyare was on the point of opening the spiritual door of the sacred place of Tsari in southern Tibet, he approached the lake of the turquoise turtle. The protecting spirit of the lake transformed itself into a turtle as big as a yak and blocked his path. His companions were taken aback, but Tsangpa Gyare leapt onto the back of the turtle. 'Let those who wish to test themselves against the spiritual heirs of the glorious lineage of the thunder dragon (*drukpa*) show themselves,' he cried, and danced on the animal's back. Immediately, the turtle changed into a boulder. Tsangpa Gyare crushed the rock with his hands and feet as if it were made of clay, bringing the life force of the spirit under his sway. He entrusted it with the protection of that

he began to sing the invocation of Padmasambhava, the Lotus-Born Guru:

> O master born from a lotus, arise with
> your retinue of dakinis!
> Buddha of the three times, turn your
> mind to us! From the ten directions
> of space . . .

As he continued his invocation, the monks were suddenly filled with inspiration and performed an exquisite dance, with movements never seen before. At the end of the chant they stopped, as if awakening from a dream. The master said: "Such an occurrence is very rare. In the future train in these dances and learn them perfectly."

Sudden inspiration can have unexpected consequences. When Chogyur Lingpa, a great visionary of the nineteenth century, was a young monk, he was performing in a festival. He started to have a vision in which he saw Padmasambhava dancing. Chogyur Lingpa immediately started to imitate the movements. The monks who were following him were confused and got their steps all wrong. This hardly ever happens and is considered to be gross negligence. Chogyur Lingpa said nothing about his vision and was obliged to leave the monastery. It was only much later that he explained the reason for his "improvised" dance.

There are many cases of this sort, which indicates that the main source of Tibetan sacred dances is meditative visionary experience.

Into Exile from the Land of Snows

It was Minling Terchen (1646–1714) and his brother, Minling Lochen (1654–1718), the founders of the famous monastery of Mindroling in central Tibet, who initiated the observance of the dances of the tenth day. Subsequently other monasteries, such as Shechen, Dzogchen, Kathok, Payul, and Dorje Trak, adopted the tradition. And now most monasteries of the Nyingma school in India perform sacred dances to celebrate the festival of the tenth day (*tsechu* in Tibetan) every year. In Tibet, during the extremely limited liberalization of the 1980s, it was possible to reestablish the dances in a few monasteries, including Shechen, whose daughter monastery in Nepal provided most of the pictures for this book.

The fifth Dalai Lama (1617–1682) sent three of his closest disciples to the province of Kham in eastern Tibet. Each one was charged with the task of founding a Nyingma monastery. One of them, Rabjam Tenpai Gyaltsen (born 1650), had a vision as soon as he arrived in Kham in which Padmasambhava instructed him to build a monastery near a white rock in the form of a lion leaping. "It will bring enormous benefits for the

Buddha's teaching," Padmasambhava added. In 1685, at the age of forty-nine, Rabjam Tenpai Gyaltsen built Urgyen Chödzong, the first monastery of Shechen, where he taught numerous disciples. He made a wish that later a great monastery would be built on the other side of the torrent, which divides the valley of Shechen.

His wish was realized by the second abbot of Shechen, Rabjam Gyurme Kunzang, who founded Shechen Tennyi Dargyeling in 1735. Shechen rapidly became one of the six principal monasteries of the Nyingma order. It was renowned for the deep spirituality of its masters and hermits and for the quality of the teaching in its school of philosophy, and also for the authenticity of its sacred arts (rituals, chants, music, and dances). Over time, some forty other monasteries would come under the spiritual authority of the mother monastery.

In 1985, when Dilgo Khyentse Rinpoche (1910–1991), one of the most remarkable spiritual teachers of the twentieth century, went back to Tibet after thirty years in exile in Bhutan and India, he found the monastery in ruins. Through his inspiration and the indomitable force of character of the Tibetans, two-thirds of the monastery has been rebuilt, and some of its activities have resumed, in spite of the cultural genocide that Tibet is undergoing. Khyentse

Rinpoche's visit was celebrated by dances involving all the monks of the monastery.

ABOVE: *A great Tibetan spiritual master dances: Khyentse Chökyi Lodrö (1893–1959).*

NEXT DOUBLE PAGE: *A procession in Tibet.*

PAGE 24: *Young monk during the dance festival of Shechen monastery, Tibet.*

PAGE 25, ABOVE: *A monk carries telescopic horns six meters long in front of the partly restored ruins of Shechen monastery.*

PAGE 25, BELOW: *Musicians practicing in the monastery square.*

These dances were an important annual event in the life of Shechen, until the Chinese occupation brought them to an abrupt halt in 1959. It was only in 1985 that the monks dared to revive the tradition. Most of the elder monks had spent twenty years in the *laogai*, the Chinese forced labor camps, but they could still remember the dances in every detail and were able to teach them to the younger generation. New masks and new costumes had to be made because the old brocade garments had been de-

Dilgo Khyentse Rinpoche, in Tibet for the first time after thirty years of exile.

stroyed. At the end of this first festival, after so many years of silence, Dilgo Khyentse Rinpoche gave teachings for the monks and laypeople who had come from far and wide to meet him. Some of the faces of this captivated audience were astonishingly beautiful, solid as a rock but with a freshness like a clear sky. Women brought their newborn babies, tucked in the folds of their sheepskin coats. The smoke of fragrant plants filled the air. The yaks and the horses of the visitors speckled the green slopes with a multitude of dots of black, white, and brown.

But it is in exile, in Nepal, Bhutan, and India, that the festivals of sacred dance have been able to continue without constraint. Straddling the Himalayas between Tibet and the great plains of India, Nepal has a particularly rich heritage of peoples, cultures, and spiritual traditions. The people of its mountains, the Sherpas, Tamangs, and Manangis, and the peoples of Mustang and Dolpo, are mostly of Tibetan culture and Buddhist. The religion and culture of the people of the valleys are mainly Hindu. The constant mingling of peoples and cultures has created a religious coexistence characterized by exceptional tolerance. This has allowed the monastery of Shechen in Bodhnath, in Katmandu valley, to become a haven for the development of sacred art and dance.

ABOVE: *The eight manifestations of Padmasambhava.*

PAGES 28–31: *Simple monks and great scholars, hermits and nomad shepherds, young and old, all come together to welcome back Dilgo Khyentse Rinpoche, and celebrate the dance festival in his honor.*

THE QUEST

For the supreme dancer of the adamantine magical display, who knows the purity of the objects of the senses, phenomena continually appear as the play of the primordial Buddha.

LOCHEN DHARMASHRI

IN THE WEST, we usually understand creativity to be the expression of the impulses that arise from personal subjective experience. For the contemplative this approach is not necessarily creative in its fullest sense because that subjective experience itself is limited by basic ignorance. Thus what one considers to be an original creation is often the result of exploring one's habitual tendencies and impulses that maintain the vicious circle of samsara, the wheel of existence. Innovation, as we usually understand it, does not necessarily free us from ignorance, greed, or animosity, or make us better, wiser, or more compassionate human beings.

From a spiritual point of view, true creativity means breaking out of the sheath of egocentricity and becoming a new person, or, more precisely, casting off the veils of ignorance to discover the ultimate nature of mind and phenomena. That discovery is something really new, and the intense, coherent, and joyous effort which leads to it is not based on an arbitrary and egocentric attitude. In fact, sacred art is an element of the

FOR PURE VISION

spiritual path. It takes courage to practice it, because its goal is to destroy the attachment to the ego.

In Buddhism there are two sorts of truth: relative truth, which is how we normally see things, and absolute truth, which appears when we examine the ultimate nature of reality and of our concepts. From the point of view of absolute truth, such notions as beautiful and ugly, pleasure and pain, pleasant and unpleasant, belong to the realm of relative truth, and arise from attachment to duality. That duality has to be transcended by an experience of reality and of the primordial purity of phenomena that leaves nothing but the "one taste" of enlightenment.

The Experience of Beauty

So what can we say about beauty in the light of this Buddhist point of view? One could perhaps simply say that beauty procures a sense of fulfillment, sometimes in the form of pleasure, sometimes in the form of happiness, according to the circumstances. One could also make a distinction between different levels of beauty, according to the kind of fulfillment they procure. One could define that which produces only temporary satisfaction as relative beauty and that which produces a lasting or even infinite sense of fulfillment as absolute beauty. We all know the power of fine music to "soothe the savage breast" and the sense of wholeness and peace procured by a magnificent landscape. But this type of fulfillment does not last. Ultimate beauty, on the other hand, leads to the unchanging fulfillment of enlightenment. It liberates us from ignorance, and thus from suffering.

The characteristics of relative beauty are not properties of the object observed, but are intimately related to the observer. The function of the sense faculties is simply to perceive their objects—forms, sounds, odors, etc. But on top of that basic experience the mind adds, "That is beautiful, this is ugly, this can harm me, that is good for me," and so on. It is not the object itself, the eye that perceives it, or the eye-consciousness that produces those subjective elabora-

Kangyur Rinpoche (1897–1975), a visionary master.

tions. Whether it is beautiful or ugly, an object does not in itself have the capacity to make the mind happy or unhappy. That element is added on by the mind. This is something that we can easily observe: consider how different individuals find the same person pleasant or unpleasant or find the same object beautiful or ugly. A mathematician will marvel at an equation and an engineer thrill at a machine. Those who love calm will delight in a Bach prelude or a Mozart concerto. A Buddhist sage contemplating the absolute transparence of the mind does not feel the need to seek a particular experience. He is in constant harmony with the nature of mind and phenomena. For him all forms are perceived as the manifestation of primordial purity, all sounds as the echo of emptiness and all thoughts as the play of wisdom. He does not need to distinguish between beautiful and ugly, harmonious or discordant. For him, beauty has become omnipresent and he is fulfilled all the time. As it is said, "In a continent of gold, you cannot find ordinary stones."

Ordinary beauty is not to be rejected, and is certainly a source of joy. But spiritual beauty, such as that of the face of a Buddha or spiritual master, has a different kind of value, because it inspires the conviction in us that enlightenment exists and that it can be attained. The feeling of inner joy that such beauty evokes is free from frustration. It is this beauty that sacred art seeks to express, whether it be Buddhist, Christian, Hindu, or Islamic, and whether its mode of expression is music, dance, painting, or simple contemplation. Sacred art is not just a representation of symbols and ideas. It is a direct experience of inner peace, free from attachment to the illusory solidity of the ego and the phenomenal world.

The Meaning of the Dances

Tibetan dances are full of symbolic meaning. For instance, when a lone dancer in a stag mask cuts up an effigy with a sword it is not an act of violence but symbolizes destroying the ego with the sword of wisdom. The masked dancers who chase each other in a colorful noisy riot do not represent the pursuit of demons but the movements of inner energy, which give rise to the mental activity that continually agitates our mind. The silent dance that follows symbolizes the inner calm that ensues when discursive thoughts are pacified. But a few symbolic elements like these cannot encompass the profound meaning that the dances find in the much vaster sphere of the meditation on "pure vision," the perception of the primordial purity of all phenomena, both animate and inanimate.

The Tibetan tradition is the only living tradition in which the three progressive levels in the Buddhist canon—the three "vehicles" (*yana*), Hinayana, Mahayana, and Vajrayana—are not only preserved but practiced together as a harmonious working whole. These three vehicles correspond to three fundamental aspects of the Buddha's teaching: renunciation, compassion, and pure perception.

Renunciation is the basis of the Hinayana, the basic vehicle or lesser vehicle, and consequently also the basis of the two vehicles that follow. It refers to a profound wish to free oneself not only from the present sufferings of this life but from samsara itself, the seemingly endless round of suffering of conditioned existence. That wish is accompanied by a deep sense of lassitude and dissatisfaction with samsara, and an intense disillusionment with worldly preoccupations. The practice of the Hinayana is to master one's thoughts in order to achieve mental calm (*shamatha*) and understanding of the nature of mind (*vipashyana*, penetrating insight).

Compassion is the driving force of the Mahayana, or great vehicle, a compassion founded on the comprehension that the individual self and all phenomena are free from any intrinsic reality. To take the infinite play of appearances as objective and permanent entities is a fundamental misunderstanding. That misunderstanding comes from ignorance and leads to suffering. An enlightened being, who has completely understood

the ultimate nature of things, spontaneously feels an immense compassion for those who are suffering in the grip of ignorance. Motivated by such compassion, the practitioner of the great vehicle does not desire liberation for himself alone but vows to attain buddhahood to be able to liberate all beings from samsara.

The pure vision of the Vajrayana, the diamond vehicle, is to recognize the buddha nature in all beings and the original purity of phenomena. The Buddha taught that just as oil is present in every single sesame seed, the essence of buddhahood is present in every being. Ignorance is simply being unaware of that fact. We are like the beggar who does not know that a crock of gold is buried under his hut. To tread the Buddhist path is to retake possession of that forgotten treasure, or, to use another traditional image, to rediscover the unchanging brightness of the sun when the wind has swept the clouds away.

The most remarkable feature of the three vehicles is that each stage of the gradual path is amplified by the one that follows. Like an alchemist who first changes iron into copper and then copper into gold, renunciation is enriched and magnified by universal compassion,

FACING PAGE: *Khyentse Rinpoche (1910–1991).*

which then becomes infinitely vast and profound when it is impregnated with the pure vision of the diamond vehicle. Achieving that vision is the purpose of meditation on a mandala, which is the heart of Tibetan ritual and the basis for the practice of sacred dance. Such meditation uses various techniques of visualization: the dancer has to imagine himself in the form of a deity. That deity is not a creator god or even an independent entity, but a manifestation of our ultimate nature, which is wisdom. The dancer, like the ascetic meditating in his hermitage, should also visualize the world around him as a pure land. The deities and the pure land together make up what is called a mandala.

The Mandala, the Divine Residence

Mandalas can be seen as meditation objects whose purpose is to gradually transform our way of perceiving the world until we rediscover its intrinsic purity. Externally a mandala takes the form of a diagram painted on canvas or drawn with colored powders. However, there are also three-dimensional mandalas.

A mandala is a plan representing a pure land, a palace that corresponds to a purified vision of the external world. In that palace reside the "deities," who are the reflection of a purified vision of ourselves and other beings and represent the different inherent qualities of enlightenment, such as wisdom and compassion. Beings who wander in the conditioned world of samsara are tormented by an infinite variety of sufferings because they cannot see the true nature of things. The way we usually perceive the external world, our body, and our mind, is described as "impure," in the sense that things seem to be solid entities with their own independent existence, and the self which perceives them seems just as real and solid. This ordinary vision of the world creates an automatic reflex of attachment and aversion, which in turn gives rise to negative emotions (such as anger, hatred, and jealousy) and harmful actions. The mechanism by which negative actions produce suffering and positive actions produce happiness is known as karma. Karma is not a form of retribution imposed by a higher power but a natural law of cause and effect.

In fact, the ordinary "impure" world is simply a mistaken perception. It has no reality whatsoever, like the shimmering water of a mirage or the imagined snake that turns out on closer inspection to be a coiled rope. From a relative point of view phenomena appear like dreams or mirages because of the coming together of causes and conditions.

Mandala of the forty-two peaceful deities.

But from the absolute point of view, nothing that comes from causes and conditions has an intrinsic, permanent, and real existence. That is what is meant by emptiness. Everything appears only as take is the basis of samsara. But even that error, that ignorance, is nothing but emptiness. It is just a veil, transitory and without substance. When one becomes aware of the nature of existence in this way, impure perceptions dissolve, leaving only the infinite purity of phenomena. Once one realizes that samsara is empty like a mirage, all the karmic patterns and negative emotions that maintain it disappear.

However, emptiness does not mean nothingness. It is at once the nature and the source of everything that exists. It is infinite potential. One who truly understands emptiness experiences a spontaneous unconceptualized compassion for beings plunged in samsara by their belief in the reality of the ego.

When one perceives all phenomena as pure, sense perceptions can be used on the path of enlightenment. The world is a "buddha-field." Forms and beings, whether friends or enemies, are manifestations of the deity who symbolizes enlightenment. The sound of water or of fire, or of the wind, or the cries of animals and human voices, are mantras. Thoughts are the play of enlightened consciousness, the ripples of wisdom.

To explain the symbolism of mandalas, which is intimately linked with the practice of visualization, we will take the

the play of interdependence; everything is interrelation, and nothing exists in itself or by itself.

To consider that things have a concrete existence is an error, and that mis-

example of the mandala of Padmasambhava. The dwelling of Padmasambhava
and his retinue is made of different
kinds of jewels, representing wisdom,
compassion, and the various activities of
the buddhas, which take different forms
and colors to fulfill the diverse aspira-
tions and needs of beings. The palace
forms a perfect square, symbolizing that
the absolute space of wisdom is beyond
error. The four doors signify that the
four boundless thoughts (love, compassion, joy at others' happiness, and impartiality) lead to great bliss. They also
symbolize the four activities of an
enlightened being: pacification (of ill-
nesses, wars, etc.), development (of spiritual qualities, long life, etc.), attraction
(of whatever leads to progress on the
path), and cutting short harmful activities (of creators of outer and inner
obstacles). The eight steps on either side
of each door mean that the first eight
vehicles of Buddhism lead to *atiyoga*, the
great perfection beyond effort. The four
levels of the portico above each entrance
symbolize "the four ways of attracting,"
methods by which a bodhisattva brings
beings onto the path. They are generosity, gentle words, teaching according to
the needs of each being, and acting in
accordance with what one teaches.

The wheel above each portico is the
Wheel of Dharma, which turns eternally.
The four pillars of the portico symbolize
the four basic methods to increase good

and overcome evil: preventing evil from
arising, controlling the evil which has already arisen, creating good, and making
the good which already exists increase.
The four rooms situated in the upper
story of the portico symbolize the four
types of meditative absorption: with
interest, with diligence, with vigilance,
and with reason. The walls of the palace
consist of five transparent layers of different colors. They symbolize the five
wisdoms: the wisdom of the absolute
nature, mirror-like wisdom, the wisdom
of perfect equality, all-distinguishing
wisdom, and all-accomplishing wisdom.
These wisdoms are the purified aspects
of the five poisons: ignorance, hatred,
pride, desire, and jealousy. The walls
also symbolize the five factors of purification: faith, effort, attention, concentration, and discernment. The five-
leveled structure between the walls and
the roof represent the five strengths that
prevent the five purifying factors from
degenerating. The ornaments of swags
and filigrees of precious substances,
flowers, silken tassels, mirrors, crescent
moons, and yak-tail fly whisks symbolize
the seven factors of enlightenment; the
eight pillars represent the eightfold path;
the eight ornamental arrangements
between the pillars and the beams are
the eight aspects of liberation; the main
beams are the four fearlessnesses that
arise when one gives up self-interest for
the sake of others; the twenty-eight sub-

sidiary pillars are the eighteen types of emptiness and the ten transcendent perfections: generosity, discipline, patience, courage, concentration, wisdom, means, prayer, strength, and primordial wisdom.

The roof represents the inconceivable qualities of enlightenment. The pinnacle symbolizes that all the inconceivable mandalas of the buddhas are included in the space of enlightened mind.

On the four sides of the roof are canopies, parasols, standards, and banners, which symbolize respectively: the purity of the absolute nature, the sense of responsibility that protects all beings, great compassion, and victory over ignorance. Little bells ring out the sound of emptiness. Dazzling rays of light emanating from every part of the palace are a sign of the infinite deployment of the body, speech, and mind of the Buddha. Entirely translucent, made of light, without the slightest shadow, the palace has "neither inside nor outside," which means that phenomena are only the play of wisdom.

The palace sits on two crossed scepters, or *vajras,* which symbolize original indestructible wisdom whose nature is emptiness. The twelve points of these two vajras symbolize the twelve interdependent links: ignorance, karmic formations, consciousness, name and form, sense faculties, contact, sensation, craving, grasping, becoming, birth, and old age and death. The sun-disk above the double vajra symbolizes the light of the absolute nature; the lotus upon which the sun rests symbolizes that this nature is perfectly pure.

The eight cemeteries that surround the palace represent the pure aspects of the eight consciousnesses: the ground consciousness, the five sense-consciousnesses, the consciousness linked to the negative emotions, and the intellectual consciousness. They also symbolize the eight similes which illustrate the illusory nature of phenomena: like a dream, a bubble, a mirage, the reflection of the moon in water, an optical illusion, an echo, a city of *gandharvas,* and a magical show. The surrounding fence of vajras represents the indestructibility of primordial wisdom, which is beyond all concepts. Finally, the wisdom-fire that surrounds the whole mandala signifies that ignorance and all the other obscurations of the mind are destroyed forever.

We can see that no detail of the mandala is there by chance. Each one has a precise symbolic meaning that the practitioner should bear in mind. Meditating on a mandala is not entering a dream world, taking an imaginary stroll through an enchanted paradise that has nothing to do with reality. On the contrary, it is the rediscovery of the very nature of our being and the phenomenal world. The aim is not to escape from reality, but to reveal it just as it is. It is not inventing futile new concepts and forms of deities, but a way of understanding the unity of appearances and emptiness. It is not cutting oneself off from others but a way of awakening limitless compassion for all beings who have forgotten that the buddha nature dwells within them.

The Symbolism of the Deities

The body of Padmasambhava represented in this painting on canvas has the indestructible nature of vajra, or diamond. He appears as an eight-year-old

FACING PAGE: *Guru Padmasambhava and his entourage, as they are described in a visionary text revealed by Jamyang Khyentse Wangpo (1820–1892). Painting on canvas known as a* thangka. *The traditional artist employs all his faculties in the service of his art, but he does not give free rein to his imagination by inventing new forms. Tibetan art is essentially anonymous, and the personality of the artist is completely subordinated to the work. This does not mean that it is a static art form anchored in the past. Masters of meditation are constantly enriching it with elements drawn from their visionary experience. Tibetan artists are often expert in the art of the miniature. It is said that in a day's work a careful miniaturist will finish about the area of a fingernail.*

child, with all the radiance of youth, which symbolizes immortality. His nine robes represent the nine vehicles of the Buddhist teaching. They include the three monastic robes, symbolizing mastery of the lesser vehicle; a blue coat, symbolizing mastery of the great vehicle, the path of the bodhisattvas; and a brocade cape, symbolizing mastery of the secret teachings of the diamond vehicle. His face represents the one absolute truth; his two arms the union of wisdom and means, or of emptiness and compassion; his two legs the sameness of samsara and nirvana in ultimate reality. His eyes are wide open and look straight ahead into space, which means that he is always aware of the absolute nature. He sits with the right leg slightly stretched forward and the left leg folded inwards in the posture known as "royal ease," to indicate that, as he is the king of wisdom, all the worlds of samsara can only follow his instructions. In his right hand he holds a five-pointed vajra, which symbolizes the transmutation of the five poisons—desire, hatred, ignorance, jealousy, and pride—into five wisdoms. In the palm of his left hand, placed in his lap in the gesture of equanimity, he holds a skull filled with nectar and topped by a vase of immortality, which means that the wisdom of Padmasambhava is beyond birth and death.

He wears a lotus hat, whose five petals symbolize the five Buddha families—

Buddha, Vajra, Ratna, Padma, and Karma. The hat also signifies that, like the lotus that rises immaculate from the mud, Padmasambhava appeared spontaneously in this world, unsullied by the birth process. On the crown of the hat are a sun and moon, symbolizing wisdom and means, topped by a vulture feather, which represents the highest view of the great perfection, or *dzogchen*, the highest teaching of Tibetan Buddhism. "Perfection" in this case means that the mind, by its very nature, innately contains all the qualities of enlightenment. Mind's empty nature is the absolute body of the Buddha (*dharmakaya*); its radiant expression is the body of spiritual delight (*sambhoga-kaya*); its omnipresent compassion is the body of manifestation (*nirmanakaya*). "Great" means that this perfection is the basic reality of whatever exists.

In the crook of his arm, Padmasambhava holds a trident, or *khatvanga*, whose three prongs symbolize the empty nature of all things, its expression, which is clear light, and omnipresent compassion. Infinite light-rays emanate from his body in the ten directions of space. Padmasambhava does not have a material, tangible body made of flesh, blood, and bone but a body of light, vivid and translucent like a rainbow, and totally immaterial, like the reflection of the moon in water. It is not just a lifeless image but full of wisdom and love and the power to help beings. Padmasambhava is surrounded by an immense retinue, which is not separate or distinct from him, since it emanates from his mind. They have the same nature, and the same wisdom and compassion. Padmasambhava himself said:

"The infinite peaceful and wrathful deities and their retinues correspond to the multiplicity of the methods needed to transform beings. Since in essence all deities have one 'taste' it is enough to meditate on the deity of your choice. In fact, although different deities express different aspects, to practice one or a great number comes to the same thing.

"If you attain realization through the practice of one deity you have also accomplished all the others. Understand that you yourself and the deity are one, and that the deity is nothing but the unborn absolute body. If, on the other hand you fabricate a deity with your dualistic attachment to subject and object, you will alternate between feelings of attachment and aversion, and that is a serious mistake."

FACING PAGE: *Arya Tara, who vowed to be reborn as a woman until she attained the enlightenment of buddhahood. She is the incarnation of the activity and compassion of all the buddhas of the past, present, and future.*

THE MONKS

On the indestructible floor of
diamond emptiness,
The heruka, through his dance
of threefold compassion,
Manifests as form in the sphere
of existence.
Homage to the illusory dancer
of Great Bliss!

LOCHEN DHARMASHRI

A GREAT TIBETAN monastery like Shechen always includes three main parts: (1) the monastery itself, where monastic life goes on, with its performance of rituals, sacred music, and dance, and where the novice monks receive their basic education; (2) a monastic college, where the monks follow a program of higher philosophical studies that can last as long as twelve years; and (3) a retreat center, where, as a culmination of their spiritual training, monks and nuns can retire from the world to devote themselves exclusively to contemplation.

The essence of Buddhism is the union of wisdom and compassion. Through wisdom we can recognize our true nature, and through compassion we come to understand that the happiness and suffering of others is more important than our own. Buddhism is also a science of the mind that addresses itself to the deepest causes of conflict and unhappiness—those that come from within ourselves. The Buddha's teaching is not a subject for intellectual curiosity; it is only useful if it is put into practice.

WHO DANCE

Buddhism is a road to enlightenment, a way to achieve liberation through intense spiritual effort. Right from the start it seeks to make us understand the mechanisms of happiness and suffering. It shows us the influence of the negative emotions that disturb us, so as to free us from them and lead us to unchanging inner joy.

The heart of the Tibetan universe is the lama, the spiritual master. One of the greatest spiritual masters of our age was Dilgo Khyentse Rinpoche (1910–1991), a master among masters who was one of the teachers of the present Dalai Lama. His inner journey had led him to a rare depth of understanding and he was a wellspring of love, wisdom, and compassion for everyone who met him. His life was the living example of what he taught. He founded Shechen monastery in Nepal and was the inspiration for all its activities, of which the most important was teaching. Khyentse taught all the time, in every available moment, giving of himself tirelessly to all those who asked for instruction or advice.

Life in the Monastery

The teaching has three phases. First there are initiations, or empowerments, whose purpose is to give the student the capacity to practice meditative techniques. Depending on the spiritual capacities of the candidates these initiations are given openly to a large audience, or to a small selected group. Then come the commentary on texts and explanations of contemplative practices, which can sometimes take several weeks. Finally there are the particular instructions given to individuals according to their needs.

The monastery has a large library with thousands of volumes. In Tibet, most of the books were destroyed during the cultural revolution. Certain texts have totally disappeared, and others only exist in a handful of examples. Shechen monastery has set itself the particular task of preserving ancient manuscripts that have been saved and reprinting important texts which are at risk of disappearing, so that they can become accessible to all.

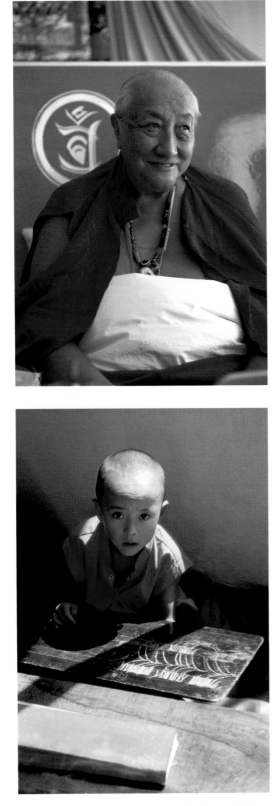

Khyentse Rinpoche (1910–1991). Through his inspiration many children have received an education at the monastery. Now it is the turn of Khyentse Rinpoche's young incarnation, Urgyen Tenzin Jigme Lhundrup (facing page), born in 1993, to pursue his studies.

The atmosphere of the monastery is open and full of life. There are old monks but also many young novices. Eighty of the two hundred residents are children or teenagers. The abbot, Rabjam Rinpoche, the seventh Rabjam since the founding of Shechen and the grandson of Khyentse Rinpoche, is still in his thirties. Among his many tasks he presides over the education of the young incarnation of his teacher, Khyentse Yangsi Rinpoche.

An important part of the role of the monastery is the training of young people to enable them to engage in a religious or scholastic vocation. From the age of six, they learn to read and write the different forms of Tibetan script. The novices have a busy schedule. They get up at half past five, and start the day with group prayers. Then they have breakfast and lessons begin. Apart from the midday meal and a few breaks, their studies continue uninterrupted until evening prayers at five o'clock. This rhythm only changes when there are special teachings in the main temple, or for the yearly and monthly ceremonies. The schedule may seem tough, and the children rarely see their families, who often live several days' journey from the monastery. Nonetheless, these children display an astonishing strength of character and joie de vivre.

At fifteen they can choose a particular direction for their future. This decision is taken with the help of their school-

master and the abbot of the monastery. They can either continue their studies in the monastic college; or they can join the ranks of the regular monks and participate in the daily ceremonies and rituals; or they can choose a more contemplative life, either within the monastery, or in secluded mountain retreat centers; or if they prefer they can leave the monastery entirely and rejoin the lay community. The actual monastic vows are only taken at the age of twenty, so they still have time to choose their final orientation. In the school of traditional arts attached to the monastery it is possible to learn painting, weaving, the making of costumes and masks, and so forth. All this provides a context in which the art of sacred dance naturally finds its place.

Master of the Dance

In the calm cool of the evening, in the middle of the vast monastery courtyard, fifty or so young monks rehearse the dances which accompany and conclude the grand ritual, under the watchful eye of the dance master, sitting on the marble steps of the monastery, indicating the rhythm with gentle taps of his cymbals. They will continue their training in the dim lamplight until late at night. To coordinate their movements they count the steps in a slow recitative. The boy-monks are often enthusiastic spectators,

and sometimes imitate their elders in a corner of the courtyard. When it is their turn to learn, they will already know most of the dances by heart. Once or twice a year the monks' prowess is tested in the presence of the abbot and the dance master. They are marked on their capacity to memorize the movements and their expressiveness, and, in the case of some dances, on their sheer athleticism.

Drudi is a dance master. He came from Tibet to transmit his knowledge of this art to the young monks of Shechen in Nepal. While continuing to watch his students out of the corner of his eye, he explained the basic principles of what makes *cham* a "dancing meditation."

"As in any spiritual practice, the dancer has to apply three essential points. Firstly he should prepare himself beforehand by having the right motivation, which means to have the 'mind of enlightenment,' the wish to attain enlightenment for the benefit of all beings. Secondly, when he dances he should be perfectly concentrated, with an awareness that all phenomena are like dreams. His mind should be clear, watchful, serene, free from attachment, and conscious of the illusory nature of things. With his body, he should faithfully represent the positions and expressions of the deities of the mandala. As the fifth Dalai Lama explains: 'The dancer should flourish the tails of his robe like a great *garuda* gliding through the firmament, and shake his hair like a snow lion shaking its turquoise mane. His body should have the grace of a tiger gliding through the Indian jungle; his trunk should be straight, his waist should form an elegant curve; his calves should be elastic, his elbows and knees fast-moving, his footwork elegant, and every movement of his body should be ample and majestic, full of ease and grace, precise and clearly defined.'

"It is also said that the dancer should move as if his feet were drawing a lotus on the ground, and that his movements should be like the wing-beats of an eagle. The symbols that the dancers hold are often in the form of weapons symbolizing the combat of enlightenment against ignorance and the victory of serene clarity over the whirlwind of emotions. The terrible laughter and song put to flight the legions of Mara, the demon who embodies attachment to the notion of self, the belief in the reality of oneself and phenomena.

"But it is not only the body that dances. The dancer must recite mantras without interruption. And in his mind, he must clearly and undistractedly visualize the deity that he is representing. He should not consider that visualization as a mere mental fabrication, but feel with pride that he *is* the deity, at the most fundamental level. He should not be attached to appearances, but be con-

ABOVE: *Drudi, the dance master who came from Tibet to teach at the monastery of Shechen in Nepal.*

FOLLOWING DOUBLE PAGE: *Some ceremonies, like this one in Shechen monastery in Nepal, continue for seven days and nights without interruption.*

scious that the various activities of body, speech, and mind take place within absolute truth, the emptiness which is the ultimate and unchanging nature of all things.

"A good dancer should not only know the meaning of the dances he is performing, but also have a real experience of meditation. So it is not surprising that the best dancers are often spiritual masters. When such masters take part in the dances their spiritual maturity can be clearly seen in the grace and power of their movements. It has been reported that at the monastery of Shechen in Tibet there was one monk who represented the wrathful deities (which symbolize a form of compassion) with such force that the audience would tremble as soon as he came onto the dance floor.

"Some repetitive dances, like the 'root dance' of the Nyingma school, which is performed in the temple by twenty-one black-hatted dancers, can go on for as long as five hours without interruption. In such cases it is not the dance which changes, but the dancer!

"The third point is that once the dance is over, it is indispensable that the dancer should dedicate the merit of what he has done so that he himself and all beings in the universe may be liberated from suffering and its causes and attain buddhahood. It is said that to dedicate the merit of one's acts in this way

is like pouring a drop of water in the ocean: It will last as long as the ocean itself. But spiritual practice which is not dedicated to help beings is like a snowflake falling on a hot stone: It evaporates right away."

Rituals

The richness and vigor of the Tibetan religious tradition can be seen in its sumptuous rituals, which often last all day. In a type of annual ceremony known as a *drupchen* the ritual continues day and night nonstop for nine days and nine nights. A ritual is a call to reflection, contemplation, prayer, and meditation. If one examines its content, the actual texts that are recited, it is a veritable guide to the themes of Buddhist meditation, such as emptiness, love, and compassion. A ritual is a spiritual practice which, carried out in the inspiring environment of a monastery whose serene atmosphere is reinforced by the sacred music, helps to free the mind from discursive thoughts and bring it to a contemplative state. The deep-voiced chanting of the liturgy is interspersed with bursts of musical offerings, mingling the sounds of long trumpets, bells, drums, and cymbals.

There are also long moments of silence, during which the participants interiorly recite mantras, sacred formulas which have a subtle effect on the mind.

For these grand ceremonies a mandala is created which represents the pure land of a divinity. It is drawn by the monks in meticulous detail, using colored powders. At the end of the ritual the mandala is swept away, symbolizing the impermanence of all things. The powders are gathered up and thrown in the river, so that all who use the water, animals or humans, may be blessed.

Sometimes the ceremonies end with dances which serve as a visual teaching, in which the world is transformed, negative forces subdued, and beings awakened to their ultimate nature and freed from suffering. Every hour in the monastery is considered precious, whether it is spent in study, in performing rituals, in contemplation, or just laughing together. Each day brings a new enrichment and leads a little further toward perfection, at the same time helping to maintain the continuity of universal values and truths which are essential not only for the Tibetans but for the whole of mankind.

RIGHT: *A* torma *is made of flour and colored butter. According to the circumstances, it can symbolize the deity and his palace, an offering, or a spiritual weapon to remove obstacles.*

Sacred Craftsmanship

The monastery is not only a place of study and contemplation. It is also a haven for the practice of traditional Tibetan art. All crafts linked to the fashioning of the accessories for dances and rituals have a sacred quality, since each object is charged with symbolism. The costumes, masks, and headdresses are not simple articles of clothing; their function is to render inner qualities visible outside. The magnificence of the music and the surroundings are not a vain display of luxury, but a reminder of the splendor of meditation and of the primordial purity of phenomena.

The meaning of the different masks, for instance, can be interpreted at a number of levels. Masks with a peaceful expression symbolize the serenity of wisdom, while the masks with a wrathful or passionate expression represent the mental poisons by which we are enslaved.

At a deeper level, the different expressions represent the purified form of the mental poisons: thus hatred becomes the "mirror-like wisdom" that transcends the division between self and others; desire is the "wisdom which comprehends the multiplicity of phenomena," that can identify the different modalities of happiness and suffering; ignorance is "the wisdom of perfect equality" that transcends all duality. From the absolute

ABOVE: *More than a hundred different masks have been made at the monastery. The majority are made from layers of glued cloth. Others are made of wood or beaten copper.*

FACING PAGE: *The procession of monks carrying the powders to draw the mandala form a* gakhyil, *or "circle of joy" (similar to the Chinese yin-yang sign).*

point of view the various different expressions of the masks symbolize that emptiness is the ultimate nature of appearances.

More than a hundred different masks are used in the various sacred dances. They have been made in Shechen monastery by Bhutanese sculptors who are among the most skilled representatives of the art. The best masks are made of successive layers of cloth which are pasted onto a carved clay mold. When the piece is dry the mold is removed and the features of the face are emphasized and refined, using red-hot metal spatulas. Then the mask is delicately painted. Sometimes hair and ornaments are added. Masks can also be carved in wood, but in that case they are heavier to wear. Some, like those of the dakinis who invoke the blessings of the Buddhas, are made of beaten copper. A mask

will only be worn once or twice a year and the rest of the time it will be stored away in the monastery treasury.

Certain ancient masks are considered precious relics, charged with blessing. An example is the mask of an aspect of Guru Rinpoche made by Pema Lingpa (1450–1521) which is still preserved in Bhutan.

Putting on a mask often requires the help of one or two assistants. It has to be firmly tied on with leather thongs so that it will remain firmly in place during the sometimes violent movements of the dance. Little protective cushions are strategically placed inside to make the mask more comfortable and keep it from rubbing against the dancer's face. The mask is three times larger than a human head. It must be positioned very precisely when it is put on because the only way for the dancer to see is through two

small holes at the corners of the mouth.
It is remarkable that, with such limited
visibility, the dancers are able to syn-
chronize their movements with such
precision, even in the most complex and
acrobatic dances.

The costumes are worn over the
monastic robe. They are made of multicolored brocades and silks traditionally
woven in China or in Benares, India. At
Shechen, the costumer, a smiling old
monk, has personally created, cut, and
sewn the monastery's hundred and fifty
costumes and headdresses. In the 1980s,
Dilgo Khyentse Rinpoche, who was
seeking ways to revive the Shechen
dance tradition, asked him if he would
be able to make costumes. He replied
that he had never done anything like
that before, but he would do his best,
since he could remember clearly and in
detail the costumes he had seen and
used in the Tibet of his youth. To everyone's astonishment, he tailored a hundred costumes, each one as perfect as
the others. Later, when some original
costumes were brought from Tibet, it
was possible to see that they were just
like the ones that he had made. This
same monk has also made a series of
ceremonial hats for the dancers and
masters of the ceremony.

*Wangchen Dorje, the old monk who made more than
one hundred dance costumes in brocade.*

ABOVE: *Rabjam Rinpoche, the present abbot of the various monasteries of Shechen, here wearing the black hat of the master of the ceremony.*

PAGE 65: *The oboes, or rgya-ling, are always played in pairs.*

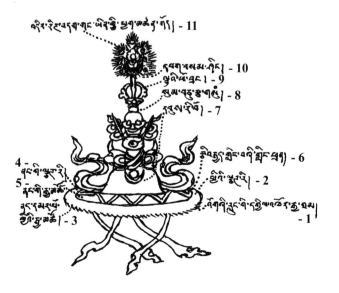

BELOW LEFT: *The black hat that is worn by twenty-one dancers for the dance known as "the golden libation," is in itself a symbol of the whole mandala. The base of the hat (1) represents the mandala of wind which supports the universe. The outside border of the brim (2) is the ring of iron mountains surrounding the universe and containing the great outer ocean (3). The inner border (4) is the ring of mountains which surrounds the inner ocean (5). The eight angles (6) of the octagon drawn with five-colored threads on the brim are the four continents and the four subcontinents. The main part of the hat (7) is Mount Meru, the axis of the world, on whose summit is the realm of the thirty-three gods, represented by the nucleus of a vajra (8). The branches of the half-vajra on top of it (9) are the palace of the gods. The crest of peacock feathers (10) is the wish-fulfilling tree, to which is attached a symbol of the principal deity of the mandala (11).*

Sacred Music

Instrumental music and chant play a major role in the rituals and dances. According to the circumstances, the music is an offering, an invocation, a call to prayer, a way of maintaining the rhythm, or a support for meditation. Playing this music, like the practice of sacred dance, is an apprenticeship in "pure vision," through which all sounds are perceived as mantras whose ultimate nature is emptiness. In this sense, sacred music liberates by hearing and is an aid to spiritual progress.

The melodies are normally passed on directly from master to disciple. There are nonetheless numerous manuscripts containing musical notation to supplement the memory of the musicians.

As Mireille Helffer explains in *Mchod-rol, les Instruments de la musique tibétaine*: "The notation serves to explain graphically the relative pitch and the different kinds of attack and extinction of the sounds, the phrasing, and the dynamics (the transitions from piano to forte or fortissimo). They remain vague about the timing, since the only indications are the adjectives 'long' and 'short.' It is not possible to play a piece of music using these notations alone. They can be used only in combination with the oral tradition. The execution of the piece depends primarily on the practical knowledge acquired by observing and copying a more experienced player." Thus the notation provides basic reference points and indications, but an apprenticeship with a qualified music-master is indispensable.

The sound of Tibetan religious music has a powerful effect. Performed in the serene atmosphere of a temple, the gentle rhythm of the monks' chant maintains the flow of contemplation; then a sudden explosion of sound fit to rouse the dead awakens the clarity of the visualization. Mireille Helffer describes the instruments that are used:

"All the schools of Tibetan Buddhism use the same instruments. Some, which are part of the Indian heritage, like the handbell (*drilbu*) or the little hourglass-shaped drum (*damaru*) are considered as ritual objects which produce sound rather than as true musical instruments. They express the harmonious play of wisdom (*shes rab*) and means (*thabs*), which correspond to emptiness and compassion, respectively. The heavy thud of the large drums (*rnga*) contrasts with the brilliance of the cymbals, which are of two main types: the heavy cymbals with a large central cavity (*rol mo* or *sbug chal*) whose sound is said to please the wrathful deities, and cymbals with a small central pommel known as 'sweet-sounding' (*sil snyan*), whose crystalline sound is more suitable for the peaceful deities. These cymbals play a central role in structuring the tempo, and accompany melodies, chants, and ritual dances. In addition to these indispensable elements there are various wind instruments, which are always played in pairs. They are:

"Conch shells (*dung dkar*), pierced at the end to form a mouthpiece; the sound of the conch is considered auspicious. They are used for summoning to prayers and to denote the peaceful character of a ritual.

"Short trumpets, originally made from a human thigh-bone, which gives them their name, *rkang gling*, literally 'leg flute'; they are now usually made of metal, and the shape of the bell of the instrument can vary considerably. They are used for short sequences in rituals of a wrathful character.

"The spectacular telescopic metal trumpets, known as *dung chen* (literally, 'great conches') or *rag dung*, ('bronze conches'), which can exceed three or four meters in length. The modulations of the three basic sounds that they produce can be used to create more extensive compositions, which are set down in special manuals (*dung tshig*).

"Oboes (*rgya- ling*), with a wooden tube pierced with seven equidistant holes on the top and one hole below. They are always used with the technique of circular breathing, making it possible to emit a continuous sound without pausing for breath. In this technique the cheeks are puffed up to store a supply of air and this air is blown into the instrument using only the cheek muscles while breathing in through the nose. In that way the players can make a continuous sound with almost no interruptions, sometimes for as long as an hour (for instance when they play to accompany a blessing given by a great lama to a large number of people)."

The
Great Cycles
of the Dance

DANCES FOR THE END OF THE YEAR

TWO HUNDRED monks strong, Shechen monastery is the setting for two great dance cycles every year. These dances are linked to ritual observances: the first takes place around February, on the last days of the year according to the Tibetan calendar. Its purpose is to remove obstacles for the coming year. In fact the dances complement a ritual that goes on for a week. On the two last days dances blend with the ritual, which becomes more and more elaborate. The dances follow one after another in the course of the day in an unchanging sequence.

The second cycle is the festival of the tenth day, a spiritual and artistic celebration in honor of the eight manifestations of Padmasambhava, danced by a hundred or so monks to an audience of thousands of devotees. It is preceded, on the ninth day of the lunar month, by a public rehearsal without masks or costumes.

The Drum Dance

THIS DANCE, performed by twenty-one dancers in black hats, originates from the first sacred dance performed at Samye, the first Tibetan monastery, founded by King Trisong Detsen and Guru Padmasambhava in the ninth century. The drum is a symbol and a reminder of the deep drumroll that resounded in space after the enlightenment of the Buddha under the bodhi tree, two thousand years ago, proclaiming the victory of wisdom over the darkness of ignorance. The Buddha saw that if there is suffering it must have a cause and thus a remedy. Addressing ignorance itself he said: "Oh jailer, for how many lives have you kept me in the prisons of birth and death? Now I have unmasked you. No longer can you build your walls around me." He had become the awakened one, having discovered a truth which is "profound, peaceful, unconditioned, luminous, and free from fabrications of the intellect."

The Golden Libation

ABOVE: *In the temple, two monks dress.*

THE TWENTY-ONE dancers have large black hats bearing a sun and moon. They wear a silver mirror on their chests and costumes of brocade hung with multicolored scarves. They have black aprons blazoned with a wrathful face. Brandishing silver cups, they make offerings to the peaceful and wrathful deities to remove obstacles on the path of liberation. Through the blessings of this dance, the monastery courtyard is as though paved with jewels and the place becomes the paradise of the glorious copper-colored mountain, the mandala of Padmasambhava. All the participants become male and female deities.

The Lords of the Cemeteries

THE CEMETERIES that the monks visualize for this dance are situated at the eight cardinal points of the mandala, and symbolize the purification of the eight aspects of consciousness, as well as the eight similes that illustrate the illusory nature of phenomena. They are the dwelling-places of the dharma-protectors who have vowed to watch over

the Buddha's teaching and those who practice it. Four dancers wearing white costumes representing skeletons carry an effigy or *linga*, which represents the ego, the attachment to the reality of a self. The consciousness of all the negative forces is concentrated into the effigy. During one of the dances that follow, the master of the ceremony liberates this consciousness by dissolving it in the space of emptiness, which is absolute truth. When the flesh and blood of ignorance have been devoured by emptiness, there remains only the pure skeleton of clear awareness, the nonduality of enlightenment which transcends fear. The skeleton is also an incitement to spiritual practice, as a reminder of the impermanence of all things.

The Separation from the Protecting Deities and the Dance of the Four Gatekeepers of the Mandala

TWO DANCERS, one wearing an owl mask, the other a crow mask, separate the effigy (*linga*) from its protecting deities. Then enter four guardians who have the heads of a vulture, a lion, a crane, and a wolf, representing the "four limitless thoughts:" love, compassion, joy at others' happiness, and impartiality. These thoughts are limitless because they are applied to limitless beings and because the benefits they bring are without limit. The vulture, who stands straight and impassive, yet remains alert, is a symbol of the stability of meditation,

and it is he who holds the *linga* in place. The lion represents analytical meditation, and he extracts the good qualities contained in the *linga*. The crane symbolizes the capacity of consciousness to elevate itself to higher states of being. The third action accomplished by the master of the ceremony is liberating the consciousness of this being filled with negative intentions. At the end it is the wolf, who consumes whatever he finds, that cuts the *linga* to pieces, so that the consciousness, once liberated, cannot come back.

The Stag Dance

AFTER THAT, in certain monasteries, the stag dance is performed.

A dancer with a stag mask performs a sacrificial dance that annihilates the ego, symbolized by an effigy. It is said that one day Padmasambhava saw the spirit of the god of the wind, riding on a stag, and stealing the minds of meditators by distracting them from the object of their concentration. Padmasambhava subdued the spirit, and mounting his stag, made him promise to protect beings.

The stag dance is also associated with the story of Palkyi Dorje, who, in the sixth century, assassinated Lang Darma, the tyrant who persecuted Buddhism in Tibet. Lang Darma had already had a large number of monks executed. On the day of a festival, Palkyi Dorje, who was an extraordinary dancer, displayed his skill under the windows of the king. He had hidden a bow in the wide sleeves of his costume. In the midst of his whirling he shot an arrow, mortally wounding the despot. In the ensuing confusion he fled, riding on a white horse which he had blackened all over with soot. When he crossed a river on his escape route, the horse became white again. At the same time he turned his black coat inside out, which was lined with white. This trick enabled him to escape his pursuers and he spent the rest of his life in a hermitage in Amdo, the northeast of Tibet.

The Dance of Yamantaka

IN THIS DANCE Yamantaka, the wrath-ful aspect of Manjushri, the buddha of wisdom, is surrounded by the assembly of deities of his mandala. The ritual continues with a series of sequences in which the master of the ceremony takes part, along with twenty-one black-hat dancers and the assembly of monks. The culmination of this ritual is when the *torma*, as the ultimate weapon for destroying all the obstacles yet to come, is cast into the fire.

LEFT AND FACING PAGE: *Rabjam Rinpoche leading the end of year ceremonies.*

A Historical Dance: The Abbot, the Master, and the King

HALFWAY between theater and dance, the representation of *Khen Lop Chö Sum* (the Abbot, the Master, and the King) retraces the coming of Buddhism to Tibet in the ninth century, when King Trisong Detsen invited first the Indian abbot, Shantarakshita, and then Guru Padmasambhava to establish the teachings of dharma in the land of snows. Usually it is the monks who perform the dances, but here it is the male and female spiritual teachers and young incarnate lamas who bring back to life this historic event.

LEFT: *The young Choling Rinpoche in the role of a prince.*

FACING PAGE: *Dilgo Khyentse Rinpoche in the role of Padmasambhava.*

THE FESTIVAL
OF THE TENTH DAY

THE SECOND annual festival of Shechen monastery, and the most grand, is one of the great events of the year. It takes place in Nepal in March or April, on the tenth day of the second lunar month, and in Tibet in June or July, on the tenth day of the fifth month. In Tibet devotees come on foot and on horseback, often with their tents and cooking utensils, and camp for several days around the monastery. In Nepal an influx of mountain-dwellers from the Himalayas jostles with inhabitants of the Katmandu valley to form an audience of thousands. The dance festival is the culmination of a long ritual lasting several days and nights, in which monks, nuns, and laypeople practice together in the temple from dawn to dusk. Then the monks take turns for the nightly vigil, so that the prayer, ritual, and meditation are never interrupted. To conclude this intense meditation the monks dance for two days in the monastery courtyard in the presence of several thousand spectators. For the community that lives in symbiosis with the monastery the festival is also a chance to meet the spiritual teachers who attend. "Their expectancy and implicit faith, their spontaneous reactions and emotions, seem to create a kind of integrated consciousness, in which performers and spectators are merged and lifted up to a level of spiritual experience that otherwise would have been unattainable and inaccessible to them."

The Seven-Line Prayer

AS WE HAVE SEEN, the original inspiration for the dance festival of the tenth day was a vision of Guru Chöwang in the twelfth century. It starts with the demarcation of the boundaries of the mandala, performed by the wrathful deities (above), and continues with the "rain of blessings," in which eight dakinis in copper masks sing the melodious seven-line prayer to invoke the blessing of Padmasambhava. It is said that, like a mother who hears her child crying, Padmasambhava cannot refuse the call of this prayer.

The Death of the Ego

THEN FOLLOW the dance of the golden
libation, which we have already described, and two dances (*gsum rgnam*
and *tshogs len*) that depict the liberation
or "putting to death" of the ego. This is
the liberation of the negative forces in
the space of absolute truth, a liberation
that takes the form of a ritual killing: an
effigy representing attachment to the
ego is dismembered by the dagger of
transcendent wisdom.

The Dance of the Sixteen Heroes

ABOVE AND FOLLOWING DOUBLE PAGE: *For the public rehearsal the dancers have no masks or costumes but wear brightly colored scarves over their monastic habits.*

THE SYMBOLISM of this dance is particularly deep and complex. It concerns the spiritual energies linking the mind and the body. The sixteen "heroes" (*ging*) represent the sixteen types of "essence" (*bindu*) whose movements in the subtle channels (*nadi*) bring about transformations in the vital "breath" (*prana*). The multicolored fans on either side of their masks signify that they are surrounded by rainbow light. Their tiger-skin skirts symbolize the sublimation of ordinary passions. The three flags on top of their

masks represent the three jewels: the
Buddha, the dharma (his teaching),
and the sangha (the community of his
followers).

The interaction between the *gings* and
their assistants, the *tsoklen*, takes the
form of a riotous pursuit in which the
dancers weave and turn in every direction amid raucous whistles. It can be
interpreted on a number of levels. The
basic meaning is the manifestation of
emptiness and compassion. On another
level the wild pandemonium is an intro-

duction to the terrifying hallucinations,
lights, and sounds that are experienced
after death, in the *bardo*, the interme-
diate state before the next rebirth. If one
can recognize that all those manifestations are just projections of the mind,
one will be liberated. A master said to a
disciple who seemed bored by the long
dances, "You'd better watch now,
because that's what you'll see at the
moment of death."

The Comic Interlude of the *Atsaras*

CURIOUSLY ENOUGH, the sacred dancers are accompanied by clowns, known as *atsaras*. These familiar stock characters are much appreciated by the crowd. For all their facetiousness, they fulfill several important functions. Firstly they are "divine madmen," like the great yogis of India, the *mahasiddhas*. Often the sons of kings, ministers, or wealthy merchants, the mahasiddhas were sometimes artisans or musicians, sometimes great scholars. Realizing that ordinary activities were no more useful than the husk of a grain of mustard seed, they discarded luxury and riches

like spit in the dust. They left home to sit at the feet of spiritual masters and live the life of a wandering hermit. In order to progress rapidly in their understanding of the illusory nature of phenomena, they would completely abandon conventional behavior and act in ways that were eccentric, disconcerting, and sometimes degrading. That is how they earned the name "divine madmen."

The function of the clowns is also to entertain the spectators during the pauses in the dances (which can be quite long, especially when a large num-

ber of dancers are involved). They also keep order, as the crowd tends to spill over into the space reserved for the dancers. Patrolling up and down the sides of the courtyard, they send unruly spectators back to their places with all sorts of antics, to everyone's great amusement. They are on hand to help the dancers tighten a mask that is slipping, or fix a costume that is coming undone, or pick up a fallen ornament. But the dancers get their share of the gags too, since the clowns do not hesitate to make fun of them and parody their dancing. "The effect is astonishing," says Lama Govinda in *The Way of the White Clouds*. "Far from destroying the atmosphere of wonder and sacredness, the juxtaposition of the sublime and the ridiculous rather seems to deepen the sense of reality, in which the highest and the lowest have their place and condition each other, thus giving perspective and proportion to our conception of the world and of ourselves."

The clowns introduce a note of good humor and amiable detachment typical of the Tibetan people, in what is at the same time a profound meditation. "Seriousness and a sense of humor," continues Govinda, "do not exclude each other; on the contrary, they constitute and indicate the fullness and completeness of human experience and the capacity to see the relativity of all things and all 'truths' and especially of our own position."

Flying Monks

THIS WHIRLING acrobatic dance is inspired by the great master Pema Lingpa's vision of the paradise of Guru Rinpoche in the fifteenth century. Pema Lingpa described it thus: "At the summit stood the palace of light, radiant with the brilliance of primordial wisdom and vast as the sky. In the center of the palace, in a space of shimmering dots and lattices of rainbow lights, sat Padmasambhava, union of the buddhas of the past, present, and future. He was surrounded by a retinue of male and female deities, dancing with myriad movements and singing the profound teachings of the great vehicle with melodious voices. The myriad deities formed a splendid cloud, accomplishing the benefit of beings in inconceivable ways."

The Drum Dance of Drametse

THE SAGE and scholar Kunga Gyaltsen, a descendent of the great Bhutanese visionary Pema Lingpa, also had numerous visions of Padmasambhava. In one of these, he visited the glorious copper-colored mountain, the "pure land" of Padmasambhava that symbolizes the pure aspect of the phenomenal world. In the course of a ritual feast, the knowledge-holders surrounding Padmasambhava metamorphosed into 108 peaceful and wrathful deities, and performed a majestic symbolic dance. After that vision, Kunga Gyaltsen added texts revealed by other visionary masters to what he had seen himself, and wrote a text in twenty-one chapters describing a dance that is regularly performed in Bhutan.

The Eight Manifestations of Padmasambhava

THE HIGH POINT of the two days of dances is the representation of the eight manifestations of Padmasambhava, a historical dance celebrating the coming of Buddhism to Tibet (see pages 8–9). In the course of his activities for the benefit of beings Padmasambhava took on different appearances, such as a buddha, a king, a yogi, or a learned sage, and also at times appeared in terrifying forms to remove obstacles on the path. The most important of those manifestations are known literally as the "eight names" of Padmasambhava. They symbolize eight spiritual experiences or eight aspects of enlightenment. In *Crazy Wisdom*, Chögyam Trungpa says: "Actually, the eight aspects are not really lineal, successive levels of development. What we have is more a single situation with eight aspects—a central principle surrounded by eight types of manifestation. There are eight aspects of all kinds of situations."

The dance of the eight manifestations is the most intense moment of the festival, a spectacle in which almost two hundred monks take part. A thrill goes through the crowd of waiting devotees as Padmasambhava, accompanied by King Trisong Detsen and the abbot Shantarakshita and flanked by his two principal spiritual consorts, Yeshe Tsogyel,

queen of Tibet, and the Indian princess Mandarava, emerges from the temple. He is followed by the eight manifestations and an immense procession. He takes his seat on a throne in the middle of the courtyard, beneath a parasol of many-colored silks. The public come to prostrate to him and his retinue, and offer white ceremonial silken scarves. When everyone has finally filed past, in an atmosphere reminiscent of the mystery plays of the Middle Ages, the eight manifestations dance, one after another, ending with the two wrathful manifestations. In *Padmasambhava, the Magic of Enlightenment*, Philippe Cornu describes the eight manifestations as follows:

Pema Gyalpo, the Lotus King

This is the aspect of Padmasambhava when he was born in a lotus, in the form of an eight-year-old child, and became the adopted son of King Indrabodhi and crown prince of the kingdom of Uddiyana. His miraculous birth in the heart of a lotus in the center of lake Dhanakosha is charged with significance for the practitioner. One of its meanings is that the buddha nature, which dwells in every being, is pure from the beginning and is born "outside time" when-

ever the yogi leaves the state of ordinary mental agitation to rest in the true nature of his mind. A lotus, the flower that springs unsullied from the mud, is the perfect metaphor for the original purity of the nature of mind, which is never muddied by the emotions.

Tsokye Dorje, the Lake-Born Diamond

After leaving his kingdom, Padmasambhava became a yogi and went to the charnel ground of Cool Grove, a terrifying place, far more gloomy and revolting than our peaceful cemeteries in the West, and demonstrated the way to transcend birth and death. Such places are ideal dwellings for tantric yogis who practice the transmutation of negative energies into wisdom through developing pure perception of whatever arises.

Shakya Senge, the Lion of the Shakyas

In his next manifestation, Padmasambhava adopts the monastic life, thus underlining the importance of the basic vehicle, or Hinayana. Shakya is the name of the clan of the historical Buddha, Shakyamuni. The proclamation of truth is compared to a lion's roar, awakening beings from the torpor of ignorance. Here Padmasambhava can be considered as a special manifestation of Shakyamuni, destined to spread the teaching of the tantras.

Nyima Özer, Rays of the Sun

Appearing in the form of a wild yogi with yellow-gold complexion and long hair gathered in a topknot, he wears a crown of five skulls and a tiger-skin skirt. He carries a trident, or *khatvanga*, in his right hand and holds the sun with a lasso of rays in his left. Stopping the sun means destroying the usual notions of time and daily routines and remaining firmly in the awareness of the present moment. This enlightened presence is beyond time; it is the "time of Samantabhadra" (the primordial Buddha), or "the timelessness of the three times."

Padmasambhava, Lotus-Born

With this name he manifested as a great pandit, or scholar of the dharma. In the garb of a doctor of philosophy, wearing a pandit's hat, he taught the philosophy of Buddhism. Simply to practice and to have spiritual experiences is not enough. In order to attain enlightenment, understanding the teaching is as necessary as practicing it. Thus study and practice are like two wings. One cannot learn to fly by developing one without the other.

FACING PAGE, ABOVE, AND PRECEDING PAGE: *The eight manifestations of Padmasambhava at Shechen, Tibet.*

FACING PAGE, BELOW: *Pema Gyalpo, the Lotus King.*

Loden Choktse, Scholar Enamored of Intelligence

This is the manifestation in which Padma (Padmasambhava) received the main tantric teachings from his eight teachers, the eight knowledge-holders of India. Subsequently, empowered by that transmission, he went to the kingdom of Zahor, where he took the princess Mandarava as his disciple.

Accused by the king of having seduced the king's daughter, Padma was condemned to be burnt alive, but his burning pyre transformed into a lake, in the middle of which Padma sat, radiant upon a lotus. Filled with remorse, the king offered him his garments and his kingdom. Padma is dressed in a royal robe. He holds aloft a small drum (*damaru*) in his right hand. In his left hand sits a skull cup filled with ambrosia. Loden Chokse is identical to Manjushri, the buddha of wisdom. He embodies the power of truth that overcomes all false accusation and censure. In fact, through the total confidence arising from the knowledge of truth, all prejudices can be overcome without unnecessary struggle: error dissolves of its own accord.

The two last names of Padma refer to his wrathful manifestations.

Senge Dradrok, the Roaring Lion

When the Buddhist pandits at Bodhgaya were seriously threatened by powerful tirthika masters (*tirthika*: "ford-makers," the name given to members of non-Buddhist religious, occult, or philosophical sects) who had challenged them to a magical combat, a dakini, who appeared as an old woman, advised them to appeal to her "brother" through prayer. Padma appeared and vanquished the tirthikas by his miraculous power. They then decided to kill him with black magic. He took on a terrifying form and, through wrathful mantras, pulverized his enemies with lightning and meteors and liberated their consciousness. Then, with a roar like a lion, he proclaimed the truth. Here the tirthikas symbolize dualistic views of good and bad and occult practices seeking personal power. Senge Dradrok is the power of truth which, like a mirror, sends evil back to its source.

Dorje Drolö, Loose-Bellied Diamond

He is the most astonishing of the eight manifestations: deep red and extremely wrathful, with three bloodshot eyes and red hair, he stands on a pregnant tigress, surrounded by flames. Padmasambhava manifested in this form in Bhutan, when he was staying at Paro Taktsang, "the tiger's lair," where he subdued the local demons and deities and hid numerous spiritual treasures, or *termas*, for the benefit of future generations.

This is the order of the eight manifestations as they are presented in texts that follow a chronological order. During this "mystery play" we see first the dance of Tsokye Dorje, followed by Padmasambhava, Pema Gyalpo, Loden Chokse, Shakya Senge, Nyima Özer, Senge Dradrok, and finally Dorje Drolö.

At the end of the leaping majestic dance of Dorje Drolö, who subdues the negative forces opposed to peace in the world, Padmasambhava, his eight manifestations, and a hundred monks enter the temple in procession in a climax of music, fluttering banners, and collective fervor. As evening approaches, the gathering of pilgrims who have shared this moment together disperse, and soon the courtyard, which reverberated with so much animation, is silent. Night falls on the calm that has suddenly returned to the monastery, calling to mind the song of Shabkar:

> When I saw the pilgrims by tens of
>   thousands
> Part from each other and disperse,
> It occurred to me that indeed this
>   showed
> The impermanence of all phenomena.
>
> Like autumn clouds, this life is transient.
> Our parents and relatives are like
>   passersby in a marketplace.
> Like dew on grass-tips, wealth is
>   evanescent.
> Like a bubble on the surface of water,
>   this body is fragile and ephemeral.

> The phenomena of the samsaric world
>   are futile;
> Only the pursuit of dharma is worthwhile.
> The chance to practice it only happens once: right now.

TEACHING DANCES OF BHUTAN

Bhutan (*'brug yul*, the land of the thunder dragon) is a Himalayan kingdom covered with lush forests and crisscrossed by clear streams. Although it is more than three hundred miles wide it has a population of less than a million. It has been unconquered and independent since the time when Vajrayana Buddhism was introduced by Padmasambhava in the eighth century. The Buddhist culture of Bhutan was further developed by Pema Lingpa, the Bhutanese revealer of spiritual treasures in the fifteenth century, and Shabdrung Ngawang Namgyal, who exercised a powerful spiritual and political influence in the seventeenth century. That culture has been able to flourish unobstructed until the present day and its values are firmly entrenched in the minds of the people. Certain great monasteries, like that of Thimphu, the capital, have more than a thousand monks.

Every hill has its little temple, surrounded by prayer flags that flutter in the breeze. The streams turn prayer wheels day and night. The mountains and forests are sprinkled with hermitages where monks, nuns, and laypeople devote themselves to meditation. The principal monasteries celebrate the festival of the tenth day, each at a different time of year, and there are a multitude of other ceremonies and dance festivals, forming a continuing series of religious celebrations all the year round.

Bhutan has been able to preserve dance traditions that were interrupted in Tibet during forty years of repression. This was the case with the following didactic dances, which were originally inaugurated by the great Tibetan visionary Karma Lingpa in the fifteenth century.

FACING PAGE: *This giant* thangka *of Padmasambhava and his eight manifestations is displayed once a year in the province of Bumthang in Bhutan. Several stories high, it is made from a patchwork of brocade sewn onto canvas.*

The Story of the Hunter

THE FESTIVAL of Thimpu, the capital, with some thirty thousand inhabitants, takes place in the vast paved courtyard of the *dzong*, the monastery fortress. A thousand monks live in one wing of the dzong; the other wing houses the ministries of the government. The festival continues for two days, and everyone, from ministers to humble peasants, wants to see it. Ritual dances are attended by the public with a sense of respectful devotion but here the dramatization of the hunter's misadventures, which illustrates the law of karma for the edification of the faithful, is received in an atmosphere of harmless fun, spiced with a touch of horror. It is the story of a hunter who has to face the consequences of his negative actions at the moment of death. In the course of the drama, he is judged by the terrifying lord of the dead, who symbolizes the infallible law of karma: positive acts lead to happiness and negative actions to suffering. In the absolute, primordial purity, which is the ultimate nature of all beings and all phenomena, transcends good and evil, happiness and suffering. But it is a disastrous mistake to imagine that, in the sphere of relative truth, one can escape from the inevitable consequences of one's actions.

The dance begins with the arrival of the lord of the dead, who enters with great pomp and takes his place on his throne. The chamberlain of the king of Bhutan and the governors of the different provinces come and offer him ceremonial scarves of white silk into which are woven the eight auspicious symbols.

Then the accused enters. His negative actions are personified by a tousle-haired demon who stamps with impatience in his eagerness to seize the dead man and drag him off to hell. With much gesticulation and menacing mimicry, he enumerates the evil deeds of the hunter, who has not only spent his life slaying animals but had also been a thorough drunkard and excellent thief, and entirely selfish to boot! The demon tallies each of his crimes with a black pebble, forming a considerable pile. Then it is the turn of the lawyer for the defense, a peaceful figure dressed in white with a white mask, who describes a few good things that the hunter has done. Once he saved six people from drowning. He did not know that what he was doing was wrong but was simply ignorant. The hunter himself expresses his

FACING PAGE, BELOW: *The white deity intercedes for the hunter.*

solemn regret: "I didn't think about the Buddha's teaching and I imagined that after leaving the body my consciousness would just disappear like the dying flame of a lamp, or a drop of water on dry ground. I thought that the notion of future lives was just talk, and so I acted without discrimination." But the pile of white pebbles cannot balance the mountain of black pebbles and the judgment is quickly decided. The workers of the lord of the dead unroll a black carpet on which they drag the condemned man by the feet to the lower realms of samsara.

The images are simplistic, perhaps, but in the simple naivety and drollery of the spectacle there is not a trace of the heavy tones of indoctrination. In spite of the way it is dramatized the underlying message is plain: we ourselves are the architects of our own destiny. There is no last judgment made by an outside entity, but it is the sum of our actions, the film of our life and our past lives, which reveals what we are. Although we cannot escape the consequence of what we have already done, we are nonetheless free to construct the future, which remains unwritten. It is also possible to compensate negative acts by positive ones before their karmic result takes effect in the form of suffering. But if we do nothing we will be the only ones to blame for what we have to go through. The combination of positive and negative actions that an individual produces is, of course, extremely complex. This

explains the mixture of joys and sorrows that we experience.

The performance has a distinctly popular touch. It rallies the faithful to virtue by means of symbols that are easily comprehensible. Thus the dancer with the head of a snake holds up a mirror in which past actions can be seen clearly without prejudice. The monkey-headed dancer weighs the good and bad actions in the pans of a scale, while an ox-headed dancer keeps tally. The dancer with the head of a garuda (mythical eagle) holds a mace to smash the rocky mountain of negative acts and a sickle to cut the root of the three mental poisons (hatred, desire, and ignorance).

It is said that this spectacle is a preparation for the hallucinations that one suffers at the moment of death through the power of karma. It is also a reminder that the wisdom and compassion of the Buddha can guide us but not take the place of our own actions. The Buddha cannot propel us to enlightenment as if he were throwing a stone, or prevent a negative action from bearing its fruit. It is up to us to give a direction to our karma and use the light of the Buddha's teachings to supplement our own lack of clairvoyance and discernment. The Buddha himself would often insist on this point: "I have shown you the way; it is up to you to follow it."

FACING PAGE: *Yama, the lord of the dead.*

The Dance of the Old Men and Women

FACING PAGE: *Monks dressed as offering goddesses, with golden tiaras and bone ornaments. In the most elaborate ceremonies, while the assembly chants the offering prayers, sixteen goddesses circle slowly around the mandala, making gestures* (mudra) *representing the different substances of offering: flowers, incense, lamps, perfume, etc.*

THERE IS ALSO a dance called "the dance of the old men and women" in which a couple, at the height of their youth and beauty, suddenly become old and decrepit. The splendor of youth lasts only a moment. The body, like all phenomena, does not last and has no essence. To be excessively attached to it only creates unnecessary suffering for oneself. The chanted text which accompanies this dance exhorts the couple to be kind to one another in the spirit of a recurrent Buddhist theme, that one should find the meaning of existence within oneself, and then radiate harmony around one in the family and the world at large.

These dances play an important role in Buddhist society. With their alternation of beauty, humor, emotion, and deep symbolism, they awaken our awareness of the fragility of existence, the swift passage of time and the importance of an altruistic attitude and an upright way of life. They do not brutalize the mind with images of violence, but stamp it with symbols of compassion; instead of fanning the flames of the passions they allow them to fade gently away in the light of serene detachment.

From Tibet to the Atlantic

ON A CLEAR WINTER MORNING, monks leap joyfully against the vast backdrop of the ocean. That evening on the stage of a theater in Brittanny, France, they would hurl themselves in the air in a cascade of rustling silks, as though borne aloft by the deep melody of the trumpets and the brilliance of the cymbals. Afterwards, coming out slowly one by one into the night, haloed with golden light, they reminded one of the verse of Rumi:

> The king of untroubled mind
> Went away, dancing

> To another land
> The land of light.

When the monks of Shechen were invited to make their first tour in France in 1995, their abbot Rabjam Rinpoche, who accompanied the troupe, had some reservations about this new challenge of presenting *cham* in the West. In fact from the very first performance of the dances it became clear that they did not come over as mere folk dance, but were able to convey in a condensed format all the essence and impact of authentic *cham*.

How can the sanctity of the performance remain intact when it takes place in a theater? Above all the answer lies in the state of mind in which the performance is offered.

Although the dancers, in their few weeks on the road, did not have time to prepare themselves with a day of prayers, and the spectators could not understand the complex symbolism of the movements, masks, and costumes, the process of transmission somehow remained intact. There was no feeling of showing off, since the monks remained quite simply themselves, and in a way it was hardly even an entertainment, but rather a shared discovery of inner peace.

There is always a link between the contemplation of the absolute and the meditation, between the meditation and the ritual, between the ritual and the dance. Without that, the dances would become useless gymnastics, an empty show with no heart.

Cham opens a window into the heart of Tibetan culture. The vision it provides of the sacred world of the monks serves as a reminder accessible to all that the extraordinary cultural heritage of the land of snows is something worth saving. The dances go on all day in the monastery and on stage the time is limited to an hour and a half, but, as the Tibetan proverb says, "The sweetness of honey does not depend on the quantity," and it is not the form of a lamp that gives light but its flame. Spiritual transmission is not a thing of the past, but still continues to maintain the living flame of enlightenment.

As long as there is space
And as long as there are beings,
May I also remain
To dispel the sufferings of the world.

SHANTIDEVA

BIBLIOGRAPHY

Works in Tibetan

Guru Chökyi Wangchuk (*gu ru chos kyi dbang phyug*, 1212–1270). *gu ru chos dbang gi mnal lam dbang skur yongs rdzogs ma zhes kyang zer rta dkar ma.* Manuscript in nine folios.

———. *rnam mthar zha nag ma.* Manuscript in twenty-seven folios.

Minling Lochen Dharmashri (*smin gling blo chen gcung chos dpal rgya mtso,* 1654–1718). *khrag 'thung khro bo'i 'chams kyi brjed byang kun bzang rnam par rtsen pa'i rol pa.*

———. *mchod gar gyi brjed byang mchod sprin rnam par spro ba'i rol mo.*

Dasho Nagphe (*dragsho nag'phel,* 1909–1976). *Lho tsan dan nags mo'i ljongs kyi 'cham yig kum gsal me long.*

Sakya Ngakchang Kunga Rinchen (*sa skya sngags 'chang'kun 'dga rin chen,* 1517–1584, the twenty-fourth patriarch of Sakya). *rdo rje phur bu dngos grub char bebs kyi 'chams kyi brjed byang snang ba 'gyur thub.* Seventy-four folios.

Works in Western Languages

Brook, E. *Chiwang Mani Rimdu.* Katmandu, 1992.

Cornu, Philippe P. *Padmasambhava, La magie de l'eveil.* Seuil: Points Sagesse, 1997.

Garcham. *The Sacred Dances of Khampagar Monastery.* Paprola, India: Tashi Jong Tibetan Community, 1992.

Govinda, Lama Anagarika. *The Way of the White Clouds.* Boston: Shambhala Publications, 1966.

Helffer, Mireille. *Mchod-rol, les Instruments de la musique tibétaine.* Paris: CNRS Editions, Editions de la Maison des Sciences de l'Homme, 1944.

Jackson, D. *A History of Tibetan Painting.* Vienna: Verlag der Österreichischen Akademie der Wissenschaften, 1996.

Khyentse Rinpoche, Dilgo. *The Heart Treasure of the Enlightened Ones.* Boston: Shambhala Publications, 1992.

Kyabgön Chetsang, Drikung. *The Snow Lion's Attributes, an Introduction to the Essence of the Drikung Vajra Dances.* (English adaptation). Jangchubling, Dehra Dun, India: Drikung Kagyu Institute, 1992.

von Nebesky-Wojkowitz, R. *Tibetan Religious Dances.* Paris: Mouton, 1976. Delhi: Pilgrim Books, 1997.

Ricard, Matthieu. *Journey to Enlightenment: The Life and World of Khyentse Rinpoche, Spiritual Teacher from Tibet.* Translated by Padmakara Translation Group. New York: Aperture Foundation, 1996

Ricard, Matthieu, et al., trans. *The Life of Shabkar.* Ithaca: Snow Lion, 2001.

Trungpa, Chögyam. *Crazy Wisdom.* Ed. Sherab Chödzin. Boston: Shambhala Publications, 1991, 2001.

ACKNOWLEDGMENTS

WE WOULD like to express our infinite gratitude to the masters who have guided and inspired us, Kyabje Kangyur Rinpoche, Kyabje Dilgo Khyentse Rinpoche, Kyabje Dudjom Rinpoche, and also Shechen Rabjam Rinpoche, to whom this work is dedicated, and who upholds the tradition of his teachers with wisdom, kindness, and courage.

Thanks also to all those who have contributed to the realization of the book through their competence, their work and their friendship, including Gene Smith, Mireille Helffer, Urgyen Chime, Christian Bruyat, Sophie Landowski, Carisse Busquet, Mark Tracy, Jill Heald, Raphaèle Demandre, Thierry Souka and Caroline Francq, and also the editors, Marion Jablonski and Jean Mouttapa, and their collaborators, Valerie Le Plouhinec, Thierry Dubreil, and Hervé Bienvault, without whom the book would never have happened.

We would also like to thank Kodak for kindly providing us with film, and Michael Hoffman, the director of Aperture, for his constant encouragement. Special thanks to Jean-Pierre Devorcine and also to Jean-Luc and Chantal Larguier and Francis Picard, through whose enthusiasm and support the monks were able to travel to the shores of Brittany, the mountains of Switzerland, and the plains of Brazil.

Finally, thanks to the monks of Shechen, who are, after all, the real authors of this book.

The photos in this work were taken with a Nikon FM 2 chassis, using 20 to 200 mm lenses, and, more recently, with a Canon EOS 5. The films used were Kodachrome 64, Fujichrome Velvia 50, and Provia 100 and 400. All photos are by Matthieu Ricard, apart from the plates on page 21 (Rigpa archives) and page 91 (Raphaèle Demandre).

Shambhala Publications, Inc.
Horticultural Hall
300 Massachusetts Avenue
Boston, Massachusetts 02115
www.shambhala.com

Previously published as *Moines danseurs du Tibet*
© 1999 by Éditions Albin Michel S.A., Paris, France
English translation © 2003 by Shambhala Publications, Inc.

9 8 7 6 5 4 3 2 1

First Shambhala Edition
Printed in France by Pollina - n° L89496.

This edition is printed on acid-free paper that meets the
American National Standards Institute z39.48 Standard.
Distributed in the United States by Random House, Inc.,
and in Canada by Random House of Canada Ltd

Library of Congress Cataloging-in-Publication Data
Ricard, Matthieu.
Monk dancers of Tibet/Text and photographs by Matthieu Ricard.
p. cm.
Includes bibliographical references.
ISBN 1-57062-974-9
1. Dance—Religious aspects—Buddhism. 2. Dance—China—Tibet.
3. Dance—Nepal. 4. Buddhism—China—Tibet—Rituals.
5. Buddhism—Nepal—Rituals. I. Title.
BQ7699.D36 R53 2003
294.3'437—dc21
2003002665